WHEN GOD HAS HAD
ENOUGH

Valerie J. Hooper

When God has had Enough
By Valerie J. Hooper
Copyright ©2017 Valerie J. Hooper

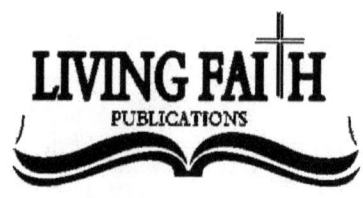

Living Faith Publications
P.O. Box 5056 • Round Rock, TX 78683

Printed in the United States of America

ISBN-13: 978-0-9973971-3-0
ISBN-10: 0997397136

All rights reserved under International Copyright Law. Contents and/or cover may not be reproduced in whole or in part, in any form or by any means, without the expressed written consent of the Publisher. Unless otherwise identified, Scripture references are taken from the NASB, NKJV and Amplified version of the Bible.

TABLE OF CONTENTS

Introduction

Chapter One…………………………….The Charges

Chapter Two……….…………….The Chastisement

Chapter Three……………...............The Conspiracy

Chapter Four………………………….The Cover-Up

Chapter Five…………………………….…..The Call

The Check-Up

TABLE OF CONTENTS

Introduction..

Chapter One.......................................The Charges

Chapter Two.................................The Insiderman

Chapter Three..............................The Awaiting

Chapter Four................................The Caught-Up

Chapter Five.....................................The Get

The Meet-Up

DEDICATION

This book is dedicated to the Lord who has prompted me to sound an alarm to alert God's people to his impending judgment for our failure to heed his voice.

I would also like to thank my husband, Bishop Calvin Hooper for encouraging me and allowing me the time needed to complete this first book project. *You're an amazing husband!*

I would also like to thank Dr. Kervin Smith for allowing the Lord to use him to prompt me to complete this project. **Procrastination is over!**

INTRODUCTION

In church, we oftentimes tend to ignore teaching from the Prophetical books, but God's words of warning to Israel, the people of God through the prophets are applicable to the Church today because we too are the people of God and we could learn a great deal of wisdom in how we live out our lives by reading and learning from the mistakes of Israel. The Apostle Paul even counsels us to learn from Israel's mistakes.

"For I do not want you to be unaware, brethren, that our fathers were all under the cloud and all passed through the sea; [2] and all were baptized into Moses in the cloud and in the sea; [3] and all ate the same spiritual food; [4] and all drank the same spiritual drink, for they were drinking from a spiritual rock which followed them; and the rock was Christ. [5] Nevertheless, with most of them God was not well-pleased; for they were laid low in the wilderness.
[6] Now these things happened as examples for us, so that we would not crave evil things as they also craved. [7] Do not be idolaters, as some of them were; as it is written, "THE PEOPLE SAT DOWN TO EAT AND DRINK, AND STOOD UP TO PLAY." [8] Nor let us act immorally, as some of them did, and twenty-three thousand fell in one day. [9] Nor let us

try the Lord, as some of them did, and were destroyed by the serpents. ¹⁰ *Nor grumble, as some of them did, and were destroyed by the destroyer.* ¹¹ *Now these things happened to them as an example, and they were written for our instruction, upon whom the ends of the ages have come.* ¹² *Therefore let him who thinks he stands take heed that he does not fall.* ¹³ *No temptation has overtaken you but such as is common to man; and God is faithful, who will not allow you to be tempted beyond what you are able, but with the temptation will provide the way of escape also, so that you will be able to endure it."*
1 Corinthians 10:1-13

If we read and study what Israel did and what the Lord had to say to them we will be less prone to fall into the same traps and sinful patterns as they did. George Santayna, a philosopher, essayist, poet and novelist once said, *"Those who cannot remember the past are condemned to repeat it."* Likewise, we should learn from Israel's mistakes so we don't repeat them today. Unfortunately, there are many in and outside of the body of Christ who apparently have not taken heed to the Word of God.

CHAPTER ONE
THE CHARGES

In the beginning of Chapter 22 of Ezekiel, the Word of the Lord comes to Ezekiel and the Lord is asking him if he will judge the bloody city, meaning Jerusalem. This appears to be repetition of the charges in Chapter 20 of Ezekiel but in that case, the charges are a historical review of the past and present and here in Chapter 22 it is an address of the present sins of the nation. The crime in the city is at an alarming rate and it is marked by violence and inhumaneness.

"Then the word of the Lord came to me, saying, And you, son of man, will you judge, will you judge the bloody city? Then cause her to know all her abominations." Ezekiel 22:1-2

Jerusalem was called the bloody city or "the city of bloods" on account of the murders committed in the city and the sacrifices of children to Molech. The phrase "bloody city" is used of Nineveh, *"Woe to the bloody city, completely full of lies and pillage; Her prey never departs."* Nahum 3:1

The Lord is asking Ezekiel to judge the city, to confront them with what they are doing by telling them what He has to say about them. *"You shall say, 'Thus says the Lord [a]GOD....*

The Lord tells Ezekiel that Israel is doing the following things to themselves.

³ You shall say, 'Thus says the Lord GOD, "A city shedding blood in her midst, so that her time will come, and that makes idols, contrary to her interest, for defilement! ⁴ You have become guilty by the blood which you have shed, and defiled by your idols which you have made. ⁶ "Behold, the rulers of Israel, each according to his power, have been in you for the purpose of shedding blood. ⁷ They have treated father and mother lightly within you. The alien they have oppressed in your midst; the fatherless and the widow they have wronged in you. ⁸ You have despised My holy things and profaned My sabbaths. ⁹ Slanderous men have been in you for the purpose of shedding blood, and in you they have eaten at the mountain shrines. In your midst they have committed acts of lewdness. ¹⁰ In you they have uncovered their fathers' nakedness; in you they have humbled her who was unclean in her menstrual impurity. ¹¹ One has committed abomination with his neighbor's wife and another has lewdly defiled his daughter-in-law. And another in you has humbled his sister, his father's daughter. ¹² In you they have taken bribes to shed blood; you have taken interest and profits, and you have injured your neighbors for gain by oppression, and you have forgotten Me," declares the Lord GOD. Ezekiel 22:3, 4a, 6-12

1) The leaders in the city are using their powers to shed blood by murdering people and instead of getting an advantage from their bloody sacrifices to idols, they have only brought the time of their punishment.

"But he who sins against me injures himself; all those who hate me love death." Proverbs 8:36

2) They are making idols and offering sacrifices on the mountain to their idols and feasting there in honor of them and committing lewd acts. The mountain shrines were the site of pagan sacrifices.

"and does not eat at the mountain shrines or lifts up his eyes to the idols of the house of Israel, or defile his neighbor's wife or approach a woman during her menstrual period." Ezekiel 18:6

3) Children, Teenagers and Young Adults are disobedient and have a lack of parental affection and admiration for parents. Respect doesn't even appear to exist.

'Cursed is anyone who dishonors their father or mother." Deuteronomy 27:16

4) There is oppression by exploiting the foreigners and mistreating the fatherless and the widow and robbing their neighbors by making unjust gain through extortion.

"Thus says the Lord, "Do justice and righteousness, and deliver the one who has been robbed from the power of his oppressor. Also do not mistreat or do violence to the stranger, the orphan, or the widow; and do not shed innocent blood in this place." Jeremiah 22:3

5) They are profaning, being disrespectful of the Sabbath, the worship service the priests that officiate the service and offering sacrifices. People are doing their own thing and neglecting the service of God which has resulted in all types of sin. The ordinances are not only neglected, but treated with contempt.

"because they rejected My ordinances, and as for My statues, they did not walk in them; they even

profaned My sabbaths, for their heart continually went after their idols. Ezekiel 20:16

6) Slanderous because people were accepting bribes to lie even when someone's life was at stake, like giving false witness in a capital case, causing bloodshed and committing fraud. This kind of economic exploitation was a direct violation of the law given in Leviticus.

"Do not take usurious interest from him, but revere your God, that your countryman may live with you." Leviticus 25:36

7) Lewdness and adultery is taking place and men are sleeping with their father's wife, violating women during their period, when they are ceremonially unclean and having sex with the neighbor's wife and their daughter-in-law. They were even violating their sisters, their own father's daughter.

[7] You shall not uncover the nakedness of your father, that is, the nakedness of your mother. She is your mother; you are not to uncover her nakedness. [8] You shall not uncover the nakedness of your father's wife; it is your father's nakedness. [9] The nakedness of your sister, either your father's daughter or your

mother's daughter, whether born at home or born outside, their nakedness you shall not uncover. ¹⁰ The nakedness of your son's daughter or your daughter's daughter, their nakedness you shall not uncover; for their nakedness is yours. ¹¹ The nakedness of your father's wife's daughter, born to your father, she is your sister, you shall not uncover her nakedness. ¹² You shall not uncover the nakedness of your father's sister; she is your father's blood relative. ¹³ You shall not uncover the nakedness of your mother's sister, for she is your mother's blood relative. ¹⁴ You shall not uncover the nakedness of your father's brother; you shall not approach his wife, she is your aunt. ¹⁵ You shall not uncover the nakedness of your daughter-in-law; she is your son's wife, you shall not uncover her nakedness. ¹⁶ You shall not uncover the nakedness of your brother's wife; it is your brother's nakedness. ¹⁷ You shall not uncover the nakedness of a woman and of her daughter, nor shall you take her son's daughter or her daughter's daughter, to uncover her nakedness; they are blood relatives. It is lewdness. ¹⁸ You shall not marry a woman in addition to her sister as a rival while she is alive, to uncover her nakedness.

¹⁹ 'Also you shall not approach a woman to uncover her nakedness during her menstrual impurity.

²⁰ *You shall not have intercourse with your neighbor's wife, to be defiled with her.* Leviticus 18:7-20

And as if that wasn't enough, lastly, but most importantly

8) They had completely forgotten all about God who had brought them out of Egypt.

> *"Beware that you do not forget the Lord your God by not keeping His commandments and His ordinances and His statutes which I am commanding you today."* Deuteronomy 8:11

> *"A voice is heard on the bare heights, the weeping and the supplications of the sons of Israel; because they have perverted their way, they have forgotten the Lord their God."* Jeremiah 3:21

> *"For Israel has forgotten his Maker and built palaces; and Judah has multiplied fortified cities, But I will send a fire on its cities that it may consume its palatial dwellings."* Hosea 8:14

There is no one to blame except themselves. They have sealed their own fate. They and they alone have brought this on themselves and now the Lord is going to make them the laughingstock of the land. Countries near and far are going to make fun of them.

"Thus you have brought your day near and have come to your years; therefore I have made you a reproach to the nations and a mocking to all the lands. 5 Those who are near and those who are far from you will mock you, you of ill repute, full of turmoil." Ezekiel 22:4b - 5

The sins which Jerusalem are charged with are extremely sinful.

"13 "Behold, then, I smite My hand at your dishonest gain which you have acquired and at the bloodshed which is among you." Ezekiel 22:13

The Lord is so upset with them that He tells Ezekiel to prophesy and smite His hands together. Merriam-Webster dictionary defines smite as: *to strike sharply or heavily especially with the hand or an implement held in the hand.* The smiting of the hands together was sometimes a sign of anger or judgment. When Balaam blessed Israel instead of cursing them,

"Then Balak's anger burned against Balaam. He struck his hands together" Numbers 24:10.

So, when the Lord saw the wickedness of Israel, his anger and judgment are expressed in the smiting of the hands together. The Lord is going to inflict a heavy blow on Israel and he will be the tool used for their punishment for what they have done.

"I will also clap My hands together, and I will appease My wrath; I, the Lord, have spoken." Ezekiel 21:17

After telling Ezekiel to tell Israel about themselves and what they've been doing he tells Ezekiel to ask them

"Can your heart endure, or can your hands be strong in the days that I will deal with you? Ezekiel 22:14.

The heart stands for the emotions so the Lord is saying, can you take the pain, the punishment that you're about to receive? You see, the Babylonians were just men, but the Lord, whom Israel had provoked to anger would be the weapon against them. **Will Israel be able to defend itself against the Lord?** No!

Israel will panic at God's judgment and so will America.

"And when they say to you, "Why do you groan?" you shall say, "Because of the news that is coming; and every heart will melt, all hands will be feeble, every spirit will faith and all knees will be weak as water. Behold, it comes and it will happen, declares the Lord God." Ezekiel 21:7

Sometimes children will do something and they think their parents forgot about it but then they hear their name being called and the parent asks, "Are you ready?" To be honest, I never liked that question. Who in their right mind would ever be ready for their punishment. But that's what the Lord asks, "Are you ready?" You did the crime, now are you ready to do the time.

The Lord basically tells them, look I've had enough of you, your time is up. I've shown you mercy, time after time, but this is it. You've been on probation, but you still haven't changed, you've only gotten worse so I can no longer withhold my judgment.

NOTES:

CHAPTER TWO
THE CHASTISEMENT

"I, the Lord have spoken and will act. I will scatter you among the nations and I will disperse you through the lands, and I will consume your uncleanness from you. You will profane yourself in the sight of the nations, and you will know that I am the Lord." Ezekiel 22:15-16

God's objective in scattering the Israelites during the Babylonian captivity was to get rid of the filth by humbling them and reducing them to a very low state. *"You, however, I will scatter among the nations and will draw out a sword after you, as your land becomes desolate and your cities become waste."* Leviticus 26:33

Their captivity was to teach them a lesson. Sometimes in life, we may go through various situations where the Lord is at work to make us better, but if we don't listen or allow the Lord's refinement to take place we can end up becoming bitter or reaping the consequences of our actions.

As a mother of five I would tell my children that they would be disciplined for some wrong they did and it seemed the longer it took me to get to disciplining them, the more they thought I had forgotten all about it. What my children failed to realize is that the discipline may have been delayed because I wanted to give them an opportunity to correct the wrong behavior and once I came to terms with their failure to change for the better I had to act. This is what the Lord did, He gave Israel an opportunity to change but they seemed to think that since the Lord was slow in dispersing punishment that He had changed His mind and wasn't going to act but we learn that the Lord has spoken and will act.

"17 And the word of the LORD came to me, saying, 18 "Son of man, the house of Israel has become dross to Me; all of them are bronze and tin and iron and lead in the furnace; they are the dross of silver. 19 Therefore, thus says the Lord GOD, 'Because all of you have become dross, therefore, behold, I am going to gather you into the midst of Jerusalem. 20 As they gather silver and bronze and iron and lead and tin into the furnace to blow fire on it to melt it, so I will gather you in My anger and in My wrath and I will lay you there and melt you. 21 I will gather you and blow on you with the fire of My wrath, and you will be melted during it. 22 As silver is melted in the furnace, so you will be melted during it; and you will know that I, the LORD, have poured out My wrath on you." Ezekiel 22:17-22

The Lord says that He's going to make Israel a laughing stock to all countries, and that they are going to be scorned (disrespected) by nations. Those near and far are going to mock them and He's going to pour out His wrath on them by melting them like silver in the furnace. Israel will know that He has poured out His wrath on them.

Precious metals are refined with intense heat to remove the impurities. So, when the metals are heated, the dross (the impurities, the worthless material) rise to the top of the molten metal and is skimmed off and thrown away because it's not good for nothing. So, the Lord is telling them that He's getting ready to put them into the fire.

At times, the Lord will put you through the furnace of affliction to burn off all your impurities, those things that don't honor and please Him and sometimes, when we really fail to heed His voice He adds some intensity to the fire. The Lord is letting them know that they've tested Him long enough and now they're going to suffer the consequences. There is no indication from Ezekiel that Jerusalem will come out of the fire as refined silver. When the Lord gets through with Israel, they are going to know it was Him.

The Lord is like the parent that gives their child an opportunity to fix their bad behavior until the parent reaches their breaking point and says, "look, I've had enough. As a child, you may have cried and your parents said, **"stop crying before I give you something to cry about!"** Maybe you didn't hear that, but I sure did and was tempted to ask my parents what they meant by that statement because I was crying because they did give me something to cry about, they had spanked my behind. And when my mom was passing out the punishment she seemed to get into a rhythm with it by saying **"Didn't – I – tell – you – not – to – play – with – knifes!"** And then she would end the punishment with **"it hurts me more than it hurts you."** You may not have experienced that, but that was my experience and as a parent I have learned what she meant. It hurts to discipline your child but you understand that if you fail to do so that you are only hurting your child by not teaching them that there are consequences for their behavior and actions.

Then the Lord comes back to Ezekiel again and says:

"23 *And the word of the* LORD *came to me, saying,* 24 *"Son of man, say to her, 'You are a land that is not cleansed or rained on in the day of indignation."* Ezekiel 22:23-24

The Lord tells Ezekiel that His judgments have been as violent floods and as the hottest fires, but Jerusalem still isn't clean.

When I think of violent floods and the hottest fires, I think of the devastation I saw in 2016 as I was traveling from the Houston, TX area and saw cattle that had been lost during a flood and the 2015 fire in Bastrop County, TX. As of the time of this writing, 2017 has been marked by deadly floods around the world in Texas, Florida, Louisiana, India, Bangladesh, Sierra Leonne, Nigeria, Nepal, Pakistan, Puerto Rico, Costa Rica, Nicaragua, Honduras, Mexico, Barbuda, Haiti, Dominican Republic and other U.S. States and Islands.

As a native of Houston, it has been hard to truly comprehend the devastation that has occurred in many parts of Houston and the surrounding areas as I watched the news reports and heard from family, friends and evacuees of the impact of the flooding that took place. I also recall the fire we had at our church facility in 2009 and remember going through items to see if anything could be salvaged and the smell of smoke that was on me for days.

Nothing has been washed away neither has anything melted out of them in the fire so because of their disobedience it's not going to rain to cool the thirsty land. This would be a mark of divine anger.

Now, before you start to judge them I imagine the Lord looking down and thinking the same thing about America. America is bringing doom on itself. How many of you know that there are consequences for ignoring the commands of God? God is forgiving, but at the same time, God is righteous and He cannot and will not ignore sin. And in case you didn't know, sin has eternal consequences and affects us both individually and collectively.

NOTES:

CHAPTER THREE
THE CONSPIRACY

By now you're probably thinking that Israel couldn't possibly do anything else wrong, but God goes on to tell Ezekiel that there is a conspiracy in the land.

²⁵"There is a conspiracy of her prophets in her midst like a roaring lion tearing the prey. They have devoured lives; they have taken treasure and precious things; they have made many widows amid her. ²⁶"Her priests have done violence to My law and have profaned My holy things; they have made no distinction between the holy and the profane, and they have not taught the difference between the unclean and the clean; and they hide their eyes from My sabbaths, and I am profaned among them. ²⁷"Her princes within her are like wolves tearing the prey, by shedding blood and destroying lives to get dishonest gain. ²⁸"Her prophets have smeared whitewash for them, seeing false visions and divining lies for them, saying, 'Thus says the Lord GOD,' when the LORD has not spoken. ²⁹"The people of the land have practiced oppression and committed robbery, and they have wronged the poor and needy and have oppressed the sojourner without justice.
Ezekiel 22:25-29

In examining the scripture passage, we learn that there are five groups involved in the conspiracy in the land. The False Prophets, the Priests, the Politicians, the Prophets and the People of the land.

The False Prophets were such a bad influence on the people for they pretended to make known the mind of God and not only did they deceive the people, but they devoured them. They lied to the people by promising peace and safety. They pursued the true prophets to discredit them and devoured those that opposed their lies. They were in conspiracy with murderers and oppressors to patronize and protect themselves in their wickedness and justify what they did with their false prophecies. They made wives into widows by giving false prophecies about the war with the Chaldeans in which the husbands fell. Their motive was greed for they would not tell their lies, without reward of something of value or money. They even took the treasure and precious things as fees for their false and flattering prophecies.

"Now in the same year, in the beginning of the reign of Zedekiah king of Judah, in the fourth year, in the fifth month, Hananiah the son of Azzur, the prophet, who was from Gibeon, spoke to me in the house of the Lord in the presence of the priests and all the people, saying, Thus, says the Lord of hosts, the God of Israel, "I have broken the yoke of the king of Babylon." Jeremiah 28:1-2

"And as raiders wait for a man, so a band of priests' murder on the way to Shechem; surely they have committed crime. Hosea 6:9

Her princes within her are roaring lions, her judges are wolves at evening; they leave nothing for the morning. Her prophets are reckless, treacherous men; her priests have profaned the sanctuary. They have done violence to the law. Zephaniah 3:3-4

"Woe to you, scribes and Pharisees, hypocrites, because you devour widows' houses, and for a pretense you make long prayers; therefore, you will receive greater condemnation." Matthew 23:14

Next on the list were the Priests. The religious leaders were just as bad as the false prophets. They didn't even call the false prophets into accountability. They violated God's law and were not teaching the people in the ways of God as they didn't make distinctions between the clean, what was lawful to be eaten and the unclean, that which was forbidden to be eaten or of the "holy" the things dedicated to God or the "profane" things that were for common use.

There was no enforcement of the Sabbath and other days, thereby endorsing the conduct of the people and allowing sin to run rampant. They basically ignored what they were seeing. They were careless and corrupt in their manner of serving in the temple. God's authority was slighted and His goodness was made light of.

"For the lips of a priest should preserve knowledge, and men should seek instruction from his mouth; for he is the messenger of the Lord of hosts." Malachi 2:7

"and to make a distinction between the holy and the profane, and between the unclean and the clean." Leviticus 10:10

Who do you think was next on the list? The Politicians, the government officials were guilty of unjust gain. Instead of fairly giving out justice and upholding the rights of the disadvantaged, they were like wolves tearing their prey. They were destroying souls by ruining families by cutting off the fathers, impoverishing the widow and the fatherless to increase their revenues or keep their position. They were even confiscating people's property.

Now hear this, head of the house of Jacob and rulers of the house of Israel, who abhor justice and twist everything that is straight, who build Zion with bloodshed and Jerusalem with violent injustice. Her leaders pronounce judgment for a bribe, her priests instruct for a price and her prophets divine for money. Yet they lean on the Lord saying, "Is not the Lord in our midst? Calamity will not come upon us." Micah 3:9-11

Then there were the Prophets. The prophets should have been God's spokesmen and denounced these wicked deeds; but (except for men like Ezekiel and Jeremiah) the prophets ignored the sins and flattered people in their ways of sin by giving the people false assurances of peace by telling the people that they shouldn't submit to the king of Babylon.

They claimed to be speaking for God when the Lord had not spoken. They were even flattering politicians in their ways of sin and violence with promises and words of encouragement. The people that had any kind of power in their hands were abusing that power.

"while they see for you false visions, while they divine lies for you to place you on the necks of the wicked who are slain, whose day has come, in the time of the punishment of the end." Ezekiel 21:29

10 It is definitely because they have misled My people by saying, 'Peace!' when there is no peace. And when anyone builds a wall, behold, they plaster it over with whitewash; 11 so tell those who plaster it over with whitewash, that it will fall. A flooding rain will come, and you, O hailstones, will fall; and a violent wind will break out. 12 Behold, when the wall has fallen, will you not be asked, 'Where is the plaster with which you plastered it?'" 13 Therefore, thus says the Lord GOD, "I will make a violent wind break out in My wrath. There will also be in My anger a flooding rain and hailstones to consume it in wrath. 14 So I will tear down the wall which you plastered over with whitewash and bring it down to the ground, so that its foundation is laid bare; and when it falls, you will be consumed in its midst. And you will know that I am the LORD. 15 Thus I will spend My wrath on the wall and on those who have plastered it over with whitewash; and I will say to you, 'The wall is gone and its plasterers are gone'" Ezekiel 13:10-15

"They have healed the brokenness of My people superficially, saying, "Peace, peace.," but there is no peace." Jeremiah 6:14

"But as for you, do not listen to your prophets, your diviners, your dreamers, your soothsayers or your sorcerers who speak to you, saying, "You will not serve the king of Babylon. "For they prophesy a lie to you in order to remove you far from your land; and I will drive you out and you will perish." Jeremiah 27:9-10

Lastly, there were the People of the land. The corruption had spread downwards through the whole community. The rich oppressed the poor, masters their servants, landlords their tenants and even parents their own children. The poor even oppressed the helpless and the consumers and the retailers even found a way to oppress one another. It was as though the Israelites had forgotten that they too had been strangers in Egypt.

"You shall not wrong a stranger or oppress him, for you were strangers in the land of Egypt." Exodus 22:21

"You shall not oppress a stranger, since you yourselves know the feelings of a stranger, for you also were strangers in the land of Egypt." Exodus 23:9

This shows just how bad things were because the leaders in the community, the people with political, spiritual and financial power and influence were corrupt. It's one thing to question politicians, but when it is joined by the faith community we are at a lost. Instead of Pastors and ministry leaders being faithful to their calling, they were placing fame, admiration, approval, acceptance, and status ahead of obedience to the Lord.

"[30] I searched for a man among them who would build up the wall and stand in the gap before Me for the land, so that I would not destroy it; but I found no one." Ezekiel 22:30

The corruption was so complete that when God searched for someone who could build up the wall, which was the hedge that would lead the people to repentance and stand in the gap to fix the breach so that He wouldn't destroy it no one could be found. There was no one within the five groups who was willing to answer the call. No one like Moses, who intervened on behalf of the people, or like Abraham who intervened for Sodom and Gomorrah.

"Therefore, He said that He would destroy them, had not Moses His chosen one stood in the breach before Him, to turn away His wrath from destroying them." Psalm 106:23

"Then Moses entreated the Lord his God, and said, "O Lord, why does Your anger burn against Your people whom You have brought out from the land of Egypt with great power and with a mighty hand?" Exodus 32:11

"He took his stand between the dead and the living, so that the plague was checked." Numbers 16:48

"²³Abraham came near and said, "Will You indeed sweep away the righteous with the wicked? ²⁴Suppose there are fifty righteous within the city; will You indeed sweep it away and not spare the place for the sake of the fifty righteous who are in it? ²⁵Far be it from You to do such a thing, to slay the righteous with the wicked, so that the righteous and the wicked are treated alike. Far be it from You! Shall not the Judge of all the earth deal justly?" ²⁶So the LORD said, "If I find in Sodom fifty righteous within the city, then I will spare the whole place on their account." ²⁷And Abraham replied, "Now behold, I have ventured to speak to the Lord, although I am but dust and ashes. ²⁸Suppose the fifty righteous are lacking five, will You destroy the whole city because of five?" And He said, "I will not destroy it if I find forty-five there." ²⁹He spoke to Him yet again and said, "Suppose forty are found there?" And He said, "I will not do it on account of the forty." ³⁰Then he said, "Oh may the Lord not be angry, and I shall speak; suppose thirty are found there?" And He said, "I will not do it if I find thirty there." ³¹And he said, "Now behold, I have ventured to speak to the Lord; suppose twenty are

found there?" And He said, "I will not destroy it on account of the twenty." ³² Then he said, "Oh may the Lord not be angry, and I shall speak only this once; suppose ten are found there?" And He said, "I will not destroy it on account of the ten." ³³ As soon as He had finished speaking to Abraham the LORD *departed, and Abraham returned to his place."* Genesis 18:23-33

No one in a position of authority in Israel had the moral qualities to lead the nation. Yes, I heard you say, "What about Jeremiah?" Jeremiah had the qualities, but he lacked the authority to lead the nation from the brink of disaster because he was forbidden to pray for the people.

"¹⁴ "Therefore do not pray for this people, nor lift up a cry or prayer for them; for I will not listen when they call to Me because of their disaster." Jeremiah 11:14

"Roam to and fro through the streets of Jerusalem, and look now and take note. And seek in her open squares, if you can find a man, if there is one who does justice, who seeks truth, then I will pardon her." Jeremiah 5:1

The United States Marine Corps has a slogan, **"The Few, the Proud, The Marines"**, but some time ago they used to have another slogan to attract recruits to the Marines. Do you know what that slogan was? **"We're Looking for a Few Good Men."** When a recruit went into the Marines, they weren't looking for them to already meet the Marine standard, but they were looking for recruits that were willing to go through whatever training was required or needed to become one of those *"Few Good Men"*. So that meant learning about self-discipline, how to submit to authority and be committed and loyal to leadership; and how to endure through hard times and maintain their integrity. Each of these qualities should be in any man or woman, not just men and women in the military. Unfortunately, the tragedy is that it often ends up being the few, not the many that meet the standard.

The main aspect of Ezekiel's ministry was that of exposing the sins, the immorality, and the injustices of the people where he lived. Can you imagine having Ezekiel's job? Ezekiel was a "watchman" and a watchman's job is dangerous. As a former soldier in the United States Army, I would be required to pull "guard duty". When your name came up on the Guard Duty roster you were responsible for guarding the camp against the enemy and you were required to memorize and know three General Orders:

The first general order was "I will guard everything within the limits of my post and quit my post only when properly relieved." Guard duty could be two hours or twenty-four hours and if you left your post without someone there to cover your post or if you feel asleep on duty you would be punished and possibly Court Martialed.

The second general order was "I will obey my special orders and perform all my duties in a military manner."

The third and final general order was "I will report violations of my special orders, emergencies, and anything not covered in my instructions to the commander of the relief."

When soldiers are on guard duty they are responsible for looking and listening for the enemy. If they fail at their post the camp might be attacked by the enemy and destroyed. Likewise, if Ezekiel failed at his post, he and the entire city might be destroyed. His own safety depended on the quality of his work. I don't imagine too many people envied his job. But how many of you would agree that we need more Ezekiel's today? We need more men and women who are willing to pull guard duty and look and listen for the enemy. And guess what, God, the Recruiter is looking.

NOTES:

CHAPTER FOUR
THE COVER-UP

30"I searched for a man among them who would build up the wall and stand in the gap before Me for the land, so that I would not destroy it; but I found no one.

In verse 30 we see that there has been a breach made in the moral state and feeling of the people so God is doing something about it and He is doing the same thing today! Do you know what He's doing? He is seeking, but what is He seeking? He is seeking men and women of God that will stand in the gap for Him, who will take sides for Him. He is looking for youth that will take a stand and represent Him. God is seeking you!

Can you believe that? He's not seeking technology, treasure or techniques, but people. He always reaches and teaches men and women through men and women. The people that God is seeking are separated. He says "I sought for a man among them." The man or woman that God is seeking is the one who is willing to come out from among those who had better things to do than serve Him.

The prophet showed that the city of Jerusalem was like a city whose walls were gapped up and broken. A gap is a breach in a wall, an opening. In ancient times, a city's defense was its walls, but the defense of Jerusalem was broken because there were great gaps in the walls. Sin makes a gap in the hedge of protection and causes decent, respectable things to run out from them and sinful, wicked things to pour into them. The city was in danger.

The prophet was not thinking about the visible and physical defenses of the city though; he was talking about the real defenses of the nation. The real defenses of any nation are not its walls or bars of iron, the real defenses of any nation are its morals, its justice, its righteousness and its wholesomeness. Not only are these things a defense for a nation, they are a defensive network for the church and the individual Christian.

The wall spoken of here is not made of stones, but of faithful people united in their efforts to resist evil. This wall was in disrepair because there was no one who could lead the people back to God. The feeble attempts to repair the gap through religious services and practices or messages based on opinion rather than God's will were as worthless as whitewash, only covering over the real problems. **It was just a cover-up**. What the people really needed was total spiritual reconstruction. They needed revival and so does America.

I propose that there are six gaps in the hedge that God has placed around America. These gaps have been caused by our carelessness to guard and uphold Biblical principles.

The first gap **IDOLATRY.** We have fallen into idolatry by worshipping our cars, television, money, sports, sex, jobs, pets, nature and many other things that keep people out of the Lord's house for worship. Anything that you allow to keep you from worshipping God becomes an idol.

The second gap is **LEWDNESS.** This is indecency, immodesty, sensuality and brazenness which points to a lack of morality. We see this on our streets, on social media, in magazines, on television, in movie theaters and sadly enough, in our churches. Growing up I loved to watch old shows like "***The George Burns & Gracie Allen Show and Father Knows Best***". If the couples weren't actually husband and wife they would be depicted sleeping in separate beds. This was a stark difference from shows today where writers are trying to change the view of family by redefining it as the ***"Modern Family"***. It started to develop slowly and subtly and before we knew it, were laughing at the shows and eventually became accustomed to them.

The third gap is **DESPISING HOLY THINGS.** This is found in defiling the temple of God which is not just limited to the church building and grounds, but to our bodies. Paul says in 1 Corinthians 6:19 *"do you not know that your body is a temple of the Holy Spirit who is in you, whom you have from God, and that you are not your own?"* People don't even attend church like they used to anymore. Other things have taken the place of attending Sunday and midweek worship services and when people do attend Sunday worship services they want to limit the Lord to thirty minutes or an hour and if the service is longer than that they will arrive late.

The fourth gap is **THE LOVE OF MONEY**. Many churches constantly face the burden of having funds to do the work of ministry, but if God's people would willingly and cheerfully give according to how God has blessed them, there would be sufficient funds to accomplish the ministry's kingdom assignment. Too often people are more concerned with building their own house rather than God's House.

The fifth gap is **FORGETFULNESS OF GOD**. In the midst of our busy schedules and making our own plans, we have simply left God out but Psalm 37:5 tells us *"commit your way to the Lord, trust also in Him, and He will do it."* How do we expect God to do something with our plans if we haven't even given them to Him?

The sixth gap is **FALSE PROPHETS** who have substituted the preaching and teaching of God's Word with relativism and humanism. If it feels right to you it must be alright. There's no such thing as sin.

Notice that when God seeks a servant He finds the person He wants. So stop asking God "why me? Or why them?" and stop making excuses for why you can't serve Him. God knows who He wants. God is looking for availability, not ability.

Let's look at a few people who God sought to use who had their share of excuses or reasons for why they felt they couldn't be used of God.

Moses gave the Lord three excuses for why he couldn't be used because of his speech.

Then Moses said the Lord, "Please, Lord, I have never been eloquent, neither recently nor in time past, nor since You have spoken to Your servant; for I am slow of speech and slow of tongue." Exodus 4:10

But Moses spoke before the LORD, saying, "Behold, the sons of Israel have not listened to me; how then will Pharaoh listen to me, for I am unskilled in speech?" Exodus 6:12

But Moses said before the LORD, "Behold, I am unskilled in speech; how then will Pharaoh listen to me?" Exodus 6:30

Gideon was called by God to be a mighty warrior even though we see him acting out of fear.

12 The angel of the LORD appeared to him and said to him, "The LORD is with you, O valiant warrior." 13 Then

Gideon said to him, "O my lord, if the LORD is with us, why then has all this happened to us? And where are all His miracles which our fathers told us about, saying, 'Did not the LORD bring us up from Egypt?' But now the LORD has abandoned us and given us into the hand of Midian." ¹⁴ The LORD looked at him and said, "Go in this your strength and deliver Israel from the hand of Midian. Have I not sent you?" ¹⁵ He said to Him, "O Lord, how shall I deliver Israel? Behold, my family is the least in Manasseh, and I am the youngest in my father's house." ¹⁶ But the LORD said to him, "Surely I will be with you, and you shall defeat Midian as one man."
Judges 6:12-16

Abraham, who was called by God to be the father of many nations but lied by saying that his wife, Sarah was his sister.

Now Abraham journeyed from there toward the land of the Negev, and settled between Kadesh and Shur; then he sojourned in Gerar. ² Abraham said of Sarah his wife, "She is my sister." So, Abimelech king of Gerar sent and took Sarah. ³ But God came to Abimelech in a dream of the night, and said to him, "Behold, you are a dead man because of the woman whom you have taken, for she is married." ⁴ Now Abimelech had not come near her; and he said, "Lord, will You slay a nation, even though blameless? ⁵ Did he not himself say to me, 'She is my sister'? And she herself said, 'He is my brother.' In the integrity of my heart and the innocence of my hands I have done this." ⁶ *Then God said to him in the dream, "Yes, I know that in the integrity of your heart you have done this, and I also kept you from sinning against Me; therefore I did not let you touch her.* ⁷ *Now therefore, restore the man's wife, for he is a prophet, and he will pray for you and you will live. But if you do not restore her, know that you shall surely die, you and all who are yours."*

⁸ *So Abimelech arose early in the morning and called all his servants and told all these things in their hearing; and the men were greatly frightened.* ⁹ *Then Abimelech called Abraham and said to him, "What have you done to us? And how have I sinned against you, that you have brought on me and on my kingdom a great sin? You have done to me things that ought not to be done."* ¹⁰ *And Abimelech said to Abraham, "What have you encountered, that you have done this thing?"* ¹¹ *Abraham said, "Because I thought, surely there is no fear of God in this place, and they will kill me because of my wife.* ¹² *Besides, she actually is my sister, the daughter of my father, but not the daughter of my mother, and she became my wife;* ¹³ *and it came about, when God caused me to wander from my father's house, that I said to her, 'This is the kindness which you will show to me: everywhere we go, say of me, "He is my brother."* ¹⁴ *Abimelech then took sheep and oxen and male and female servants, and gave them to Abraham, and restored his wife Sarah to him.* ¹⁵ *Abimelech said, "Behold, my land is before you; settle wherever you*

please." ¹⁶ To Sarah he said, "Behold, I have given your brother a thousand pieces of silver; behold, it is your vindication before all who are with you, and before all men you are cleared." ¹⁷ Abraham prayed to God, and God healed Abimelech and his wife and his maids, so that they bore children. ¹⁸ For the LORD had closed fast all the wombs of the household of Abimelech because of Sarah, Abraham's wife. Genesis 20:1-18

Paul was changed from Saul, a persecutor of the church to a preacher of the Gospel.

Now Saul, still breathing threats and murder against the disciples of the Lord, went to the high priest, ² and asked for letters from him to the synagogues at Damascus, so that if he found any belonging to the Way, both men and women, he might bring them bound to Jerusalem. ³ As he was traveling, it happened that he was approaching Damascus, and suddenly a light from heaven flashed around him; ⁴ and he fell to the ground and heard a voice saying to him, "Saul, Saul, why are you persecuting Me?" ⁵ And he said, "Who are You, Lord?" And He said, "I am Jesus whom you are persecuting, ⁶ but get up and enter the city, and it will be told you what you must do." ⁷ The men who traveled with him stood speechless, hearing the voice but seeing no one. ⁸ Saul got up from the ground, and though his eyes were open, he could see nothing; and leading him by the hand, they brought him into Damascus. *9 And he was three days without sight, and neither ate nor drank.* *10 Now there was a disciple at Damascus named Ananias; and the Lord said to him in a vision, "Ananias." And he said, "Here I am, Lord." 11 And the Lord said to him, "Get up and go to the street called Straight, and inquire at the house of Judas for a man from Tarsus named Saul, for he is praying, 12 and he has seen in a vision a man named Ananias come in and lay his hands on him, so that he might regain his sight." 13 But Ananias answered, "Lord, I have heard from many about this man, how much harm he did to Your saints at Jerusalem; 14 and here he has authority from the chief priests to bind all who call on Your name." 15 But the Lord said to him, "Go, for he is a chosen instrument of Mine, to bear My name before the Gentiles and kings and the sons of Israel; 16 for I will show him how much he must suffer for My name's sake." 17 So Ananias departed and entered the house, and after laying his hands on him said, "Brother Saul, the Lord Jesus, who appeared to you on the road by which you were coming, has sent me so that you may regain your sight and be filled with the Holy Spirit." 18 And immediately there fell from his eyes something like scales, and he regained his sight, and he got up and was baptized; 19 and he took food and was strengthened.* Acts 9:1-19

David was a shepherd working out in the fields tending sheep.

¹² So he sent and brought him in. Now he was ruddy, with beautiful eyes and a handsome appearance. And the LORD said, "Arise, anoint him; for this is he." ¹³ Then Samuel took the horn of oil and anointed him in the midst of his brothers; and the Spirit of the LORD came mightily upon David from that day forward. And Samuel arose and went to Ramah.

¹⁴ Now the Spirit of the LORD departed from Saul, and an evil spirit from the LORD terrorized him. ¹⁵ Saul's servants then said to him, "Behold now, an evil spirit from God is terrorizing you. ¹⁶ Let our lord now command your servants who are before you. Let them seek a man who is a skillful player on the harp; and it shall come about when the evil spirit from God is on you, that he shall play the harp with his hand, and you will be well." ¹⁷ So Saul said to his servants, "Provide for me now a man who can play well and bring him to me." ¹⁸ Then one of the young men said, "Behold, I have seen a son of Jesse the Bethlehemite who is a skillful musician, a mighty man of valor, a warrior, one prudent in speech, and a handsome man; and the LORD is with him." ¹⁹ So Saul sent messengers to Jesse and said, "Send me your son David who is with the flock." ²⁰ Jesse took a donkey loaded with bread and a jug of wine and a young goat, and sent them to Saul by David his son. ²¹ Then David came to Saul and attended him;

and Saul loved him greatly, and he became his armor bearer. ²² Saul sent to Jesse, saying, "Let David now stand before me, for he has found favor in my sight." ²³ So it came about whenever the evil spirit from God came to Saul, David would take the harp and play it with his hand; and Saul would be refreshed and be well, and the evil spirit would depart from him. 1 Samuel 16:12-23

God finds the person who is willing to be **AVAILABLE** for His purpose. He finds the man or woman He wants. This is the greatest need in the church today, Men and Women who are completely dedicated to God and who are available to Him for His service. We can't all teach, preach, play instruments, or hold the same offices, but by the grace of God, we can all stand for the Lord and this is exactly what He wants.

The Bible tells us in Proverbs 14:34 that *"Righteousness exalts a nation, but sin is a disgrace to any people."* A nation like America may have great wealth, but unless there are men and women who are pure in heart, living a clean life and who fear God, that's nation's defense is gapped and the nation is in great danger. In other words, the invincible hedge of any nation are not the walls, gates, guns, ships or armaments, but men and women who fear God and who are willing to place their lives on the line to glorify God.

There is another fact in the text about the kind of man or woman that God is seeking. God is seeking a man or woman that will stand before Him. God wants people that will stand in the gap before Him **FOR THE LAND!** God was seeking someone to stand in the gap so that He "should not destroy the land", because it is so corrupt. God cannot overlook sin. God has never, nor will He ever make an exception for even one sin. God cannot condone what is wrong; He must judge it because He is God. Because God must judge it, someone must stand in the gaps for Him.

What is the greatest service any of us can do for our country now or anytime? Live a pure, Christ-like life and be a man or woman of prayer and stand up for what is right against everything that is evil and wrong. God wants men and women who will spread righteousness and truth, that will counter act the forces of evil that are running wild in the world today. One thing is for sure, there is no way that anyone can stand in the gap in their own strength. It will take the strength of the Lord for a person to stand in the gap. This means that all the resources of God are available to the man or woman who will build up the wall and stand in the gap for Him. All the unlimited power that God has is there to enable us to take a stand for God in our homes, at our jobs, in our communities, at our churches or wherever we are.

NOTES:

CHAPTER FIVE
THE CALL

I believe there are great gaps in the defenses of our nation today just as there were thousands of years ago. As I watch the news and look at what is taking place I believe we are wearing God's patience thin as we continue to live in sin, never accepting God's plan for forgiveness of sin. The Lord has prompted me to write this book to let people know that **"He has had enough!"** But can I tell you it's not too late because God always provides a way out of our dilemma.

1 Corinthians 10:13 says "no temptation has overtaken you but such as is common to man; and God is faithful, who will not allow you to be tempted beyond what you are able, but with the temptation will provide the way of escape also, so that you will be able to endure it."

The Israelites had brought this upon themselves and sadly enough so has America. *"Thus I have poured out My indignation on them; I have consumed them with the fire of My wrath; their way I have brought upon their heads," declares the Lord God."* Ezekiel 22:31

"But as for Me, my eye will have no pity nor will I spare, but I will bring their conduct upon their heads." Ezekiel 9:10

"But as for those whose hearts go after their detestable things and abominations, I will bring their conduct down on their heads," declares the Lord God." Ezekiel 11:21

"Because you have not remembered the days of your youth but have enraged Me by all these things, behold, I in turn will bring your conduct down on your own head," declares the Lord God, *"so that you will not commit this lewdness on top of all your other abominations."* Ezekiel 16:43

"So, they shall eat of the fruit of their own way and be satisfied with their own devices." Proverbs 1:31

"Woe to the wicked! It will go badly with him, for what he deserved will be done to him. Isaiah 3:11

"Hear, O earth: behold, I am bringing disaster on this people, the fruit of their plans, because they have not listened to My words, And as for My law, they have rejected it also." Jeremiah 6:19

God is here and He is still looking. Have you accepted the call? Are you ready to accept the responsibility of standing in the gap and making repairs to the hedge of the Lord? God is still seeking. He is looking for men and women of God to be like Moses who stood in the gap when he made intercession for Israel to turn away the wrath of God or like Abraham, who interceded on behalf of the wicked cities of Sodom and Gomorrah, or like Daniel who took a stand for God despite the society in which he lived; like Job who remained faithful to God despite his circumstances; and like Joshua and Caleb who were courageous even though the odds were against them.

God is seeking men and women among those in America, Africa, India, South America, Canada, London, China, Korea and everywhere that should make up the hedge and stand in the gap before Him for the land that He should not destroy it. My question for you is **what will the Lord find?** If he sought your house, your community, your workplace, your church for those that should make up the hedge and stand in the gap before Him for the land that He should not destroy it would He find you? **Where do you stand?**

Those of you in positions in the church, where do you stand? Parents and Teenagers, where do you stand? Will you forsake the world and answer the clarion call of God when He says, "Whom shall we send?" Will you answer, "Here am I Lord, Send (Use) me? Will you stand in the gap and interceded on behalf of your family, your friends, the church, your workplace, schools and government officials and countries.

God has had enough and He is looking for Men and Women of God who will cry out as Ezekiel did about the sin that is so prevalent in our world today. Are you serving like the military soldier on guard duty? Are you guarding your post?

Will you heed the call today? God is looking for men and women who aren't afraid to confront and deal with sin in our society. Men and women who aren't going to just laugh at sin, but men and women who are going to take situations that they see taking place to the Lord in prayer. Men and women that are going to take a stand and call sin what it is, **SIN**.

NOTES:

THE CHECK-UP

1. Can God count on you to charge your city for the things that are taking place?

2. What are some things you have observed taking place in your city, town or State?

3. Are any of the things you've observed like what was taking place with Israel?

4. How would you feel about your city or nation being mocked by others?

5. What have you noticed about how children (pre-teens, teenagers and Young adults) are treating their parents?

6. Have you seen or heard of stories of the fatherless and widows being burdened?

7. Is there a reverence for the holy things, especially worship services?

8. Do you see people being falsely accused of crimes they haven't committed?

9. Is there such a thing as sexual decency or modesty in your community?

10. What is the state of morality today?

11. Have you heard of people taking bribes to fatten their pockets?

12. Have people forgotten God?

13. Do you feel people are prepared for God's judgment?

14. How widespread was the corruption in Israel? How widespread is the corruption in America?

15. How do you respond to the things you see taking place in your city?

16. Are you willing to intercede on behalf of your family, your community, your workplace, your city, your church, your state, your country or the world?

17. Do you know of others willing to stand in the gap?

ABOUT THE AUTHOR

Valerie Hooper, affectionately referred to as "Pastor Val," is a native of Sugarland, Texas, the wife of Bishop Calvin Hooper, and a veteran of the United States Army. Pastor Val graduated Cum Laude with a Bachelor of Business Administration degree from American Intercontinental University.

A Christian woman of virtue, poise and grace, Pastor Val is known as a teacher, administrator, leader, business woman, author, Executive Pastor, First Lady of the Household of Faith Christian Fellowship Church, fondly referred to as "The House" which she co-founded with her husband in June 2003 along with their five children.

Pastor Val openly shares from her past, including rape, low self-esteem, abuse and fear of rejection. Her passion is ministering to women who are broken and hurting and assisting them in achieving spiritual and emotional wholeness. One of her primary goals is to help women discover their God-given purpose.

She is the founder of the Designer Original Women's Conference and has touched the lives of women as she ministers to women on how the ultimate designer, Jesus Christ has fashioned them. She encourages women to appreciate the person that God has called them to be "A Designer Original." She is also the founder of Princess to Princess, an event for young girls and teenagers.

Of her many roles, Pastor Val especially cherishes that of wife to a mighty man of God and mother to five incredibly gifted children. Pastor Val continues to seek God's direction for her life as she has learned that all things are possible with Christ.

Works Cited

Blenkinsopp, J. (1990). *Ezekiel* (pp. 95–98). Louisville, KY: J. Knox Press.

Freeman, J. M., & Chadwick, H. J. (1998). *Manners & customs of the Bible* (p. 381). North Brunswick, NJ: Bridge-Logos Publishers.

Hamilton, V. P. (1995). Ezekiel. In *Evangelical Commentary on the Bible* (Vol. 3, p. 575). Grand Rapids, MI: Baker Book House.

Jamieson, R., Fausset, A. R., & Brown, D. (1997). *Commentary Critical and Explanatory on the Whole Bible* (Vol. 1, p. 595). Oak Harbor, WA: Logos Research Systems, Inc.

New American Standard Bible (NASB)
Copyright © 1960, 1962, 1963, 1968, 1971, 1972, 1973, 1975, 1977, 1995 by The Lockman Foundation

www.ingramcontent.com/pod-product-compliance
Lightning Source LLC
Chambersburg PA
CBHW051707090426
42736CB00013B/2572